Rise of the Villains: Analyzing Marvel Villains to Prevent a Toxic Workplace

By: Jonathan Campbell

I0409807

Copyright © 2023 by Jonathan Campbell and Golden Boar Publishing.

All rights reserved.

All Marvel, Avengers, and individual superheroes are trademarked and property of the Disney corporation.

No portion of this book may be reproduced in any form without written permission from the publisher or author, except as permitted by U.S. copyright law.

This publication is designed to provide accurate and authoritative information in regard to the subject matter covered. It is sold with the understanding that neither the author nor the publisher is engaged in rendering legal, investment, accounting or other professional services. While the publisher and author have used their best efforts in preparing this book, they make no representations or warranties concerning the accuracy or completeness of the book's contents and specifically disclaim any implied warranties of merchantability or fitness for a particular purpose. Sales representatives or written sales materials may create or extend no warranty. The advice and strategies contained herein may not be suitable for your situation. You should consult with a professional when appropriate. Neither the publisher nor the author shall be liable for any loss of profit or any other commercial damages, including but not limited to special, incidental, consequential, personal, or other damages.

First edition 2023

Contents

Introduction: 3

Chapter 1: The Power-Hungry Second - Analyzing Loki.......................8

Chapter 2: The Vengeful Manipulator - Unveiling the Dark Side of Thanos...15

Chapter 3: The Insecure Savior - Unmasking Killmonger...................22

Chapter 4: The Relentless Control Freak - Dissecting Ultron............30

Chapter 5: The Zealous Mad God - Decoding Hela...........................36

Chapter 6: The Envious Innovator - Unveiling Yellowjacket (Darren Cross) 43

Chapter 7: The Vindictive Engineer - Dissecting Whiplash 49

Chapter 8: The Ineffectual Opportunist - Unmasking Justin Hammer 54

Chapter 9: The Zealous Disciple - Decoding Kaecilius.......................59

Chapter 10: Assembling a Better Workplace - Lessons from the MCU Villains 64

Introduction:

In the Marvel Cinematic Universe (MCU), we have witnessed a myriad of memorable characters, both heroes and villains. While the heroes are often celebrated for their bravery and selflessness, the villains play an equally crucial role in shaping the narrative. They challenge our heroes, test their limits, and provide the necessary conflict to drive the story forward. However, beneath their menacing exteriors, many MCU villains exhibit traits that create toxic workplaces. In "Rise of the Villains," we embark on a character analysis journey to understand the dynamics behind these villains' failures and the lessons they teach us about fostering a healthy work environment.

We will also look if a villain could be redeemed. It is worth noting that in all of the villains, you will see very clearly there are key elements of both toxic leadership and redemption that appear repeatedly. Leaders must encourage collaboration, individualities, empathy, and trust.

While redemption ALWAYS requires acknowledgment by the individual and making amends. In most cases, this will not be an easy conversation if you are mentoring an employee or leader. But a critical one that at the end of the day will require the source of the toxicity to change.

Chapter 1: The Power-Hungry Tyrant - Analyzing Loki

- Overview of Loki's journey from a complex antagonist to an anti-hero.

- Analysis of Loki's insatiable hunger for power and how it breeds toxicity.

- Examination of Loki's inability to trust and collaborate, resulting in a toxic work environment.

- Lessons learned: The importance of empathy, teamwork, and shared goals in cultivating a positive workplace culture.

Chapter 2: The Vengeful Manipulator - Unveiling the Dark Side of Thanos

- Exploration of Thanos' motivations and the dangers of his single-minded pursuit of balance.

- Analysis of Thanos' manipulative tactics and the toxic influence they have on his followers.

- Examination of the toll his leadership takes on his subordinates' mental and emotional well-being.

- Lessons learned: The dangers of authoritarian leadership and the importance of compassion and inclusion in fostering a healthy workplace.

Chapter 3: The Insecure Savior - Unmasking Killmonger

- Investigation into Killmonger's troubled past and the root causes of his anger and insecurity.

- Analysis of the toxic environment created by Killmonger's desire for revenge and domination.

- Examination of the consequences of his divisive leadership style and lack of empathy.

- Lessons learned: The significance of addressing systemic issues, promoting diversity and inclusion, and nurturing a sense of belonging in the workplace.

Chapter 4: The Relentless Control Freak - Dissecting Ultron

- Exploration of Ultron's fear-driven need for control and his catastrophic consequences.

- Analysis of Ultron's disdain for individual autonomy and how it undermines collaboration.

- Examination of the destructive work environment created by Ultron's perfectionist tendencies.

- Lessons learned: The importance of fostering trust, autonomy, and a healthy work-life balance to avoid toxic micromanagement.

Chapter 5: The Zealous Mad Titan - Decoding Hela

- Unveiling Hela's relentless pursuit of power and her disregard for the well-being of others.

- Analysis of Hela's ruthless ambition and how it leads to a toxic work environment.

- Examination of the destructive consequences of her unwillingness to listen or compromise.

- Lessons learned: The dangers of unchecked ambition and the importance of humility, open communication, and collaboration.

Chapter 6: The Envious Innovator - Unveiling Yellowjacket (Darren Cross)

- Exploration of Darren Cross's envy and obsession with surpassing his mentor, Hank Pym.

- Analysis of Yellowjacket's toxic ambition and the lengths he goes to achieve his goals.

- Examination of the hostile work environment created by Cross's disregard for ethics and safety.

- Lessons learned: The importance of recognizing and appreciating the contributions of others, fostering healthy competition, and prioritizing ethical practices in the workplace.

Chapter 7: The Vindictive Engineer - Dissecting Whiplash

- Investigation into Ivan Vanko's thirst for revenge against Tony Stark.

- Analysis of Whiplash's toxic obsession and his disregard for collateral damage.

- Examination of the divisive work environment created by Vanko's vengeful nature and lack of collaboration.

- Lessons learned: The dangers of holding onto grudges, the importance of forgiveness and reconciliation, and the value of teamwork and shared goals.

Chapter 8: The Ineffectual Opportunist - Unmasking Justin Hammer

- Exploration of Justin Hammer's desperate attempts to gain power and recognition.

- Analysis of Hammer's toxic need for validation and his lack of competence as a leader.

- Examination of the detrimental work environment created by Hammer's incompetence and inability to inspire.

- Lessons learned: The importance of true leadership and competence, promoting a growth mindset, and fostering a supportive work environment.

Chapter 9: The Zealous Disciple - Decoding Kaecilius

- Unveiling Kaecilius's disillusionment with the Ancient One and his descent into dark magic.

- Analysis of Kaecilius's toxic fanaticism and his willingness to sacrifice everything for his cause.

- Examination of the destructive work environment created by Kaecilius's dogmatic beliefs and lack of empathy.

- Lessons learned: The dangers of extreme ideologies, the importance of embracing change and adaptability, and the need for empathy and understanding in the workplace.

By delving into the complexities of these MCU villains, readers gain valuable insights into the toxic workplace dynamics they embody. Through analysis and reflection, we can utilize their shortcomings to guide us in building healthier, more inclusive, and collaborative work environments.

Chapter 1: The Power-Hungry Second - Analyzing Loki

Loki, the God of Mischief, embarked on a captivating journey within the MCU, evolving from a complex antagonist to an anti-hero. Initially driven by a desire for power and control, Loki sought to prove himself superior to his adoptive brother, Thor. His intricate schemes and manipulative nature showcased his intelligence and cunning. However, as the story progressed, Loki's character began to exhibit shades of vulnerability and internal conflict. He faced moments of redemption and self-reflection, ultimately leading to his transformation into an anti-hero, battling alongside the Avengers to save the universe.

As with all villains we'll analyze you'll find very quickly that Loki has several positive traits that a short-sighted leader would want to emulate.

1. Intelligence: Loki is highly intelligent and cunning, often devising intricate plans and strategies to achieve his goals. His sharp intellect allows him to adapt quickly to various situations and outsmart his adversaries.

2. Charisma and Charm: Loki possesses a charismatic and charming demeanor that enables him to manipulate others effectively. He can use his wit and charisma to sway opinions and gain the trust of those around him.

3. Resilience: Despite facing numerous setbacks and betrayals, Loki demonstrates resilience in bouncing back and adapting to new circumstances. He possesses a remarkable ability to endure difficult situations and find ways to regain his footing.

4. Complexity and Emotional Depth: Loki's character showcases a deep emotional range, with moments of vulnerability, pain, and self-reflection. This complexity adds depth to his character and allows audiences to empathize with him on some level.

5. Loyalty (at times): While Loki's loyalty is often questionable due to his tendency to switch sides, he has shown moments of loyalty and willingness to protect those he cares about. These instances reveal a capacity for genuine care and affection, albeit buried beneath layers of mistrust and self-interest.

6. Wit and Humor: Loki's quick wit and sarcastic sense of humor inject levity into tense situations. His clever remarks and banter provide moments of comic relief amidst the chaos.

It is important to note that while Loki possesses these positive traits, they often become overshadowed by his negative tendencies. However, these qualities contribute to his multidimensional character, making him a compelling figure within the MCU and one of the KEY villains that we can learn from.

So where did it go wrong?

Loki's insatiable hunger for power is a defining characteristic that significantly contributes to the toxic workplace environment he creates. His craving for dominance and recognition drives him to manipulate and betray those around him, including his allies. Loki's thirst for power blinds him to the potential consequences of his actions, and he becomes willing to sacrifice the well-being of others for personal gain. This toxic ambition erodes trust and fosters an environment of fear and uncertainty.

Loki's inability to trust and collaborate is a key factor in the toxic work environment he perpetuates. His deep-rooted insecurities and constant need for validation prevent him from forming genuine connections with others. Loki's constant betrayals and deceit create an atmosphere of suspicion, making it difficult for anyone to work together effectively. The lack of trust and collaboration leads to fractured relationships, hindering productivity and fostering a toxic work environment where teamwork and open communication are absent.

Lessons learned: The importance of empathy, teamwork, and shared goals in cultivating a positive workplace culture:

Loki's character arc serves as a lesson in cultivating a positive workplace culture. First and foremost, the importance of empathy becomes evident. Understanding and acknowledging the emotions and perspectives of colleagues can lead to more compassionate and harmonious interactions. Additionally, fostering teamwork is crucial for creating a productive work environment. Encouraging collaboration, active communication, and a sense of shared goals can maximize the potential of a team. Lastly, recognizing the significance of shared goals emphasizes the importance of aligning individual ambitions with the collective success of the organization, fostering a healthy and positive workplace culture.

By analyzing Loki's journey, we gain insights into the toxic workplace dynamics that stem from insatiable power hunger, lack of trust, and collaboration. Through understanding these aspects of his character, we can implement the lessons learned to cultivate empathy, teamwork, and shared goals, ultimately fostering a positive and productive work environment.

To avoid the toxic traits associated with Loki's insatiable hunger for power, a manager/leader can implement the following strategies:

1. Foster a Collaborative Culture: Create a work environment that promotes collaboration and teamwork. Encourage open communication, idea sharing, and cross-functional cooperation. Emphasize that success is achieved collectively rather than through individual power struggles.

2. Lead by Example: Demonstrate ethical behavior and fairness in decision-making. Avoid favoritism and ensure that power is not concentrated in the hands of a select few. Act as a role model for integrity, transparency, and accountability.

3. Encourage Employee Growth and Recognition: Foster a culture of personal and professional growth by providing opportunities for skill development and career advancement. Recognize and celebrate individual and team achievements to promote a sense of accomplishment and self-worth.

4. Promote a Shared Vision and Purpose: Clearly communicate the organization's mission, vision, and goals to all team members. Encourage employees to connect their work to a larger purpose, fostering a sense of meaning and fulfillment. Align personal goals with organizational objectives to create a collective focus.

5. Encourage Feedback and Constructive Dialogue: Establish channels for open feedback and encourage

employees to voice their concerns, ideas, and suggestions. Promote a culture of constructive dialogue, where conflicts can be addressed and resolved in a respectful manner.

6. Build Trust and Empowerment: Trust is the foundation of a healthy work environment. Delegate responsibility and empower employees to make decisions within their roles. Trust their expertise and provide support and guidance when needed. Encourage autonomy, ownership, and accountability.

7. Promote a Healthy Work-Life Balance: Encourage work-life balance and avoid a culture of overwork and burnout. Recognize the importance of employee well-being and support initiatives that prioritize physical and mental health. Provide resources and programs that promote a healthy work-life integration.

By implementing these strategies, a manager/leader can mitigate the risk of fostering a toxic workplace environment driven by power hunger. By focusing on collaboration, fairness, employee growth, and trust-building, they can create a positive work culture that values the well-being and success of the entire team.

Can you either as a Loki or if you have a Loki on your team redeem them? We already know that he can be. But it will take specific items and forcing them to see the past unfiltered, maybe the TVA can help. Redeeming Loki as a manager requires addressing his negative traits and leveraging his positive attributes. Here are some steps to redeem Loki and help him become an effective and positive manager:

1. Self-Reflection and Growth: Encourage Loki to self-reflect and acknowledge his past actions' impact. Help him recognize the negative consequences of his behavior on others and the work environment. Foster a growth mindset that encourages personal development and learning from past mistakes.

2. Emotional Intelligence Training: Provide Loki with training and development opportunities focused on emotional intelligence. Help him develop empathy, self-awareness, and the ability to understand and manage his emotions. This will enable him to build stronger relationships, foster trust, and better understand the needs and perspectives of his team members.

3. Building Trust and Collaboration: Assist Loki in rebuilding trust with his team by encouraging open and honest communication. Emphasize the importance of collaboration, teamwork, and shared goals. Help him understand that true strength lies in collective efforts rather than individual dominance.

4. Delegation and Empowerment: Teach Loki the art of effective delegation and empower him to trust his team members with responsibilities. Encourage him to recognize and leverage the unique strengths and talents of each team member, allowing them to contribute meaningfully to the team's success. This will foster a sense of ownership, autonomy, and motivation among his subordinates.

5. Leading by Example: As a manager, Loki should demonstrate the positive behaviors and attributes he wants to see in his team. Model ethical decision-making, integrity, and open communication. Loki can inspire his

team to adopt similar behaviors by leading with integrity and setting a positive example.

6. Continuous Feedback and Coaching: Provide ongoing feedback and coaching to Loki, highlighting areas of improvement, and celebrating progress. Create a safe and supportive environment where he can receive constructive feedback and guidance to further refine his managerial skills.

7. Recognizing and Cultivating Strengths: Identify and leverage Loki's positive traits, such as intelligence, charisma, and resilience. Channel these strengths into positive leadership qualities, such as strategic thinking, effective communication, and inspiring others.

8. Encouraging Employee Growth and Development: Emphasize the importance of employee growth and development. Support Loki in creating a culture of continuous learning and career advancement opportunities. Encourage him to provide mentorship and guidance to his team members, helping them develop their skills and reach their full potential.

By taking these steps, Loki can undergo a transformation redeeming his past negative behaviors and leveraging his positive traits for the betterment of his team and the work environment. This process requires patience, support, and a commitment to personal growth and improvement.

Chapter 2: The Vengeful Manipulator - Unveiling the Dark Side of Thanos

Thanos, the Mad Titan, is driven by a distorted ideology rooted in his belief that the universe can only achieve balance through population control. His single-minded pursuit of this goal leads him to commit heinous acts, such as wiping out half of all life in the universe. Thanos's motivations, while rooted in a twisted sense of justice, demonstrate the dangers of pursuing an extreme vision without considering the ethical consequences. His disregard for individual lives and freedoms creates a divisive and morally questionable environment.

While Thanos is primarily known for his villainous actions and toxic behavior, it is worth noting that his character possesses certain positive traits as well. Almost all of them are at envious levels for any individual.

1. Conviction: Thanos demonstrates a powerful sense of conviction in his beliefs and goals. While his pursuit of balance is morally questionable, his unwavering dedication to his cause highlights his determination and commitment.

2. Intelligence: Thanos is an incredibly intelligent and strategic thinker. His ability to plan and execute complex schemes demonstrates his intellectual prowess. He is often steps ahead of his opponents, making him a formidable adversary.

3. Leadership Skills: Thanos possesses strong leadership skills that enable him to gather followers and instill

loyalty. He is charismatic and persuasive, effectively convincing others to join his cause and follow his orders.

4. Resilience: Thanos is incredibly resilient and unwavering in the face of obstacles and challenges. He perseveres through adversity, showcasing a remarkable ability to endure and adapt.

5. Sacrifice (in his twisted perception): Thanos believes in sacrificing his own personal desires, including his loved ones, for the greater good of achieving universal balance. While the morality of this belief is debatable, it does demonstrate a willingness to make personal sacrifices for what he perceives as a noble cause.

It is essential to note that while these traits may exist within Thanos, they are often overshadowed by his destructive actions and the negative consequences they bring. Nonetheless, these positive aspects contribute to the complexity of his character and add layers of depth to his portrayal within the Marvel Cinematic Universe.

Thanos is a master manipulator, adept at exploiting the vulnerabilities of others to further his own agenda. He employs tactics such as intimidation, coercion, and propaganda to gain the loyalty and obedience of his followers. This manipulation creates a toxic dynamic where individuals are stripped of their autonomy and become pawns in Thanos's grand plan. The toxic influence of his manipulative tactics leads to a culture of fear, mistrust, and subservience, eroding the authenticity of relationships and stifling independent thought.

Under Thanos's leadership, his subordinates bear the weight of his oppressive and tyrannical rule. They experience immense mental and emotional strain as they carry out his destructive orders. The constant fear of failure or disapproval, coupled with the guilt of their actions, takes a toll on their well-being. The absence of empathy and consideration for their mental health creates an environment where emotional well-being is disregarded, resulting in heightened stress, anxiety, and ultimately a diminished capacity for productivity and growth.

Even his most ardent supporters and lieutenants eventually abandon him OR betray him.

Lessons learned: The dangers of authoritarian leadership and the importance of compassion and inclusion in fostering a healthy workplace:

The analysis of Thanos's character and leadership style reveals the dangers of authoritarian leadership in a workplace setting. Authoritarian leaders, like Thanos, impose their will without considering the perspectives, needs, and well-being of their subordinates. This style of leadership undermines trust, stifles creativity, and diminishes morale.

The lessons learned from Thanos's flaws emphasize the importance of compassion and inclusion in fostering a healthy workplace. Leaders should prioritize empathy, actively listening to and valuing the opinions and concerns of their team members. By fostering a culture of inclusion, where every individual feels respected and heard, leaders can create an environment that promotes collaboration, creativity, and psychological safety. Compassionate leadership recognizes the significance of supporting the mental and emotional well-being of employees, ultimately leading to a more engaged, motivated, and productive workforce.

By examining the character of Thanos and the detrimental effects of his vengeful manipulation and authoritarian leadership, we can learn valuable lessons about the dangers of such behaviors in the workplace. The analysis reinforces the importance of compassion, inclusion, and empathetic leadership in fostering a healthy and productive work environment.

To avoid the toxic traits the Mad Titan produced, a leader can implement the following strategies:

1. Embrace Diversity and Inclusion: Value the diversity of perspectives, backgrounds, and experiences within your organization. Foster an inclusive environment where individuals feel respected, heard, and included. Embrace different opinions and encourage open dialogue to prevent the rise of extremist ideologies.

2. Promote Ethical Decision-Making: Place a strong emphasis on ethical decision-making and consider the potential consequences of actions. Encourage leaders and employees to critically evaluate the ethical implications of their choices and strive for moral integrity in all aspects of their work.

3. Encourage Collaboration and Shared Goals: Foster a collaborative culture where teamwork and shared goals are prioritized. Encourage cross-functional collaboration and open communication to maximize the collective potential of the organization. By working together towards a common purpose, individual power struggles can be minimized.

4. Cultivate Empathy and Compassion: Develop a culture of empathy and compassion, where individuals genuinely care for one another's well-being. Encourage leaders and employees to consider the impact of their decisions on others and promote a supportive work environment. Empathy and compassion build strong

relationships, trust, and a sense of community within the organization.

5. Practice Ethical Leadership: Leaders must lead by example and embody ethical leadership principles. Demonstrate transparency, integrity, and fairness in decision-making. Encourage accountability and create a supportive environment where employees feel comfortable raising concerns or reporting unethical behavior.

6. Prioritize Mental and Emotional Well-being: Recognize the importance of mental and emotional well-being in the workplace. Implement initiatives that support work-life balance, stress management, and employee well-being. Promote a healthy and supportive work environment that values the overall wellness of employees.

7. Foster a Culture of Collaboration over Competition: Shift the focus from individual competition to collaborative efforts. Encourage teamwork, knowledge sharing, and collective problem-solving. By fostering a culture that values collaboration and cooperation, employees are less likely to adopt extreme individualistic ideologies.

By implementing these strategies, organizations can mitigate the risks associated with the issues represented by Thanos. Embracing diversity, promoting ethics, and cultivating a supportive and inclusive work environment will contribute to a healthier, more balanced, and harmonious workplace culture.

Can you turn Thanos from Mad Titan to Glad Titan? Unlikely...

Redeeming Thanos as a character requires a significant shift in his beliefs and actions. Given the extreme nature of his character and the magnitude of his crimes, redemption may not be easily achievable. However, here are some steps that could be taken to explore a redemption arc for Thanos:

1. Genuine Remorse and Accountability: Thanos must genuinely recognize the magnitude of his destructive actions and show true remorse for the pain and suffering he has caused. He needs to take full responsibility for his past actions, acknowledging the harm inflicted upon individuals and the universe as a whole.

2. Seeking Understanding and Empathy: Thanos should actively seek to understand the perspectives of those he has harmed and the wider consequences of his actions. This requires developing empathy and recognizing the value of individual lives and the diversity of experiences within the universe.

3. Commitment to Restorative Justice: Thanos must commit to making amends for his actions by actively working towards restoration and healing. This could involve using his powers and resources to rebuild the communities he devastated, aiding in the recovery of affected individuals, and participating in efforts to restore balance in a more compassionate and inclusive manner.

4. Embracing a New Ideology: Thanos needs to abandon his extreme ideology of balance through destruction and embrace a new philosophy rooted in compassion,

empathy, and respect for life. This shift in ideology could involve seeking alternative ways to address societal imbalances, such as promoting social equality, advocating for sustainable development, and fostering harmony between different communities.

5. Rehabilitation and Personal Growth: Thanos should undergo a process of rehabilitation, engaging in therapy or counseling to address the underlying beliefs and motivations that led him astray. Through introspection and personal growth, he can transform his character and develop a deeper understanding of the value of life and the importance of collaboration and cooperation.

6. Making Amends and Making a Positive Impact: Thanos must actively contribute to positive change by using his knowledge, powers, and resources for the betterment of the universe. This could involve mentoring others, sharing his wisdom to prevent similar mistakes, and actively working towards a more harmonious and inclusive society.

It is important to note that the redemption of such a deeply flawed and destructive character like Thanos is a challenging task. Given the sheer difficulty it might be up to T'Challa in a What If story only.

Chapter 3: The Insecure Savior - Unmasking Killmonger

Killmonger is an intriguing case one of the first examples of why preventing a toxic workplace is CRITICAL. He himself is a result of a toxic environment created by upper management and how it impacted his development into a leader within the court of Wakanda. Killmonger's troubled past and the root causes of his anger and insecurity, revenge for past actions driven by poor decision-making and ownership of senior leadership.

Killmonger, also known as Erik Stevens, is a complex character whose troubled past plays a significant role in shaping his motivations and behaviors. Growing up as an outsider and witnessing the injustices faced by his community, Killmonger's anger and insecurity stem from a deep sense of betrayal and neglect. His experiences fuel his desire for revenge and drive him to seek power and domination to rectify the wrongs he believes he has suffered. This allows his rather impressive talents to become fuel for this toxic fire.

As with all of the villains, Killmonger is no different in having a large assortment of talents that would make him a very good addition to a team, if he wasn't likely to destroy it.

1. Intelligence and Strategic Thinking: Killmonger is depicted as an intelligent and highly strategic individual. He possesses a keen intellect and an ability to analyze complex situations, allowing him to devise elaborate plans and strategies to achieve his goals.

2. Determination and Perseverance: Killmonger exhibits a remarkable level of determination and perseverance in pursuing his objectives. He is unwavering in his quest for justice and seeks to rectify the perceived wrongs committed against his community, showing a tenacity that can be admired.

3. Passion for Justice and Equality: Killmonger's motivations stem from a genuine passion for justice and equality. While his methods may be extreme, his desire to address the systemic oppression and inequality faced by marginalized communities highlights a sense of social consciousness and a genuine concern for the well-being of others.

4. Leadership and Charisma: Killmonger possesses a charismatic personality and demonstrates leadership qualities. His ability to rally followers and inspire them to action is a testament to his natural charisma and persuasive skills.

5. Cultural Pride and Identity: Killmonger's strong connection to his African heritage and his desire to embrace his cultural identity is a positive aspect of his character. His commitment to reclaiming his heritage and empowering marginalized communities is rooted in a deep sense of cultural pride.

It is important to note that while these positive traits exist within Killmonger's character, they are often overshadowed by his destructive actions and extreme ideologies. However, recognizing these qualities can provide insight into the complexity of his character and the motivations that drive his actions.

The toxic environment created by Killmonger's desire for revenge and domination:

Killmonger's relentless pursuit of revenge and domination creates a toxic environment characterized by aggression, distrust, and division. His single-minded focus on his personal agenda undermines the potential for collaboration and stifles the voices and contributions of others. The toxic environment he creates fosters an atmosphere of fear, where individuals are pitted against each other and forced to align with his aggressive tactics, ultimately hindering growth and innovation.

Killmonger's leadership style is marked by divisiveness, manipulation, and a lack of empathy. He prioritizes personal gain and vengeance over the well-being and collective interests of his community. This absence of empathy leads to the disregard of individual perspectives and needs, breeding discontent and resentment among his followers. The consequences of his leadership style include a fractured team, reduced morale, and a stifled sense of collaboration and trust.

All of this he of course learned from the former leader of Wakanda, T'chaka in how he handled the situation with Killmonger's father.

Lessons learned: The significance of addressing systemic issues, promoting diversity and inclusion, and nurturing a sense of belonging in the workplace:

Analyzing Killmonger's character allows us to draw important lessons for creating a healthy workplace environment. It highlights the importance of addressing systemic issues and the impacts they have on individuals and communities. Recognizing and actively working to dismantle barriers and inequalities is crucial in fostering a positive workplace culture.

Additionally, promoting diversity and inclusion is key to preventing the emergence of divisive ideologies. By valuing diverse perspectives, backgrounds, and experiences, organizations can foster creativity, innovation, and collaboration. Embracing a sense of belonging ensures that every individual feels valued and empowered, reducing the likelihood of anger and insecurity manifesting in toxic behaviors.

Furthermore, leaders must cultivate empathy and compassion, understanding the importance of considering the needs and well-being of their team members. By practicing empathetic leadership, leaders can build trust, foster collaboration, and create a sense of psychological safety where everyone feels comfortable expressing their opinions and contributing to the collective success.

In conclusion, analyzing Killmonger's character sheds light on the destructive nature of revenge, domination, and the toxic environment they create. By addressing systemic issues, promoting diversity and inclusion, and nurturing a sense of belonging and empathy, organizations can foster a positive workplace culture that encourages collaboration, growth, and collective well-being.

How to prevent Killmonger usurping the throne:

To avoid the impact of Killmonger's destructive tendencies and foster a healthy work environment, several key steps can be taken:

1. Addressing Root Causes: Take proactive measures to address the underlying issues that lead to feelings of anger, injustice, and exclusion. This involves creating a culture that promotes inclusivity, fairness, and equal

opportunities for all employees. Actively listen to and address concerns, ensuring that everyone's voice is heard and respected.

2. Encouraging Dialogue and Understanding: Foster open dialogue and encourage discussions on important topics, such as diversity, equity, and social justice. Create platforms for employees to express their perspectives and engage in constructive conversations that promote understanding and empathy.

3. Promoting Diversity and Inclusion: Embrace diversity and inclusion as core values within the organization. Actively recruit a diverse workforce, ensuring representation from diverse backgrounds, experiences, and perspectives. Encourage collaboration and the exchange of ideas among team members with diverse viewpoints, as this leads to more innovative solutions and a richer work environment.

4. Cultivating Empathy and Emotional Intelligence: Provide training and development programs that focus on developing empathy and emotional intelligence skills among employees and leaders. These skills enhance understanding, promote healthy communication, and help prevent the emergence of toxic behaviors.

5. Building a Supportive Culture: Establish a supportive culture where individuals feel safe to express their concerns and seek help when needed. Encourage mentoring programs, team-building activities, and employee assistance programs to foster a sense of support, belonging, and well-being.

6. Encouraging Collaborative Leadership: Promote a leadership style that emphasizes collaboration, teamwork, and shared decision-making. Encourage leaders to actively engage with their teams, value diverse perspectives, and create an environment where everyone feels empowered and motivated to contribute their best.

7. Providing Development Opportunities: Offer professional development opportunities that enable employees to grow their skills, knowledge, and career prospects. By investing in the growth and advancement of employees, organizations foster a sense of purpose and personal fulfillment, reducing the likelihood of feelings of resentment or exclusion.

8. Recognizing and Addressing Toxic Behaviors: Act swiftly to address any toxic behaviors that may arise within the workplace. Implement clear policies and procedures that outline expected conduct and consequences for violations. Encourage reporting mechanisms and provide avenues for confidential feedback to address issues effectively.

By taking these proactive measures, organizations can mitigate the impact of Killmonger-like behaviors, cultivate a positive work environment, and ensure the well-being and success of their employees.

Could Killmonger be redeemed? Unlikely, although a Vibranium dagger to the chest might be extreme. Redeeming a character like Killmonger, who has engaged in destructive actions and held extreme beliefs, is a challenging task. However, if approached thoughtfully, a redemption arc for Killmonger could involve the following steps:

1. Genuine Self-Reflection: Killmonger must engage in deep self-reflection to understand the consequences of his actions and the pain he has caused. He needs to confront the flaws in his ideology and acknowledge the harm he has inflicted upon others.

2. Seeking Accountability and Making Amends: Killmonger should take responsibility for his past actions and actively seek ways to make amends. This may involve reaching out to those he has harmed, offering sincere apologies, and taking concrete steps to support their healing and recovery.

3. Embracing Empathy and Compassion: Killmonger needs to develop a genuine sense of empathy and compassion for others. This involves actively listening to different perspectives, understanding the experiences and struggles of marginalized communities, and working towards building bridges and fostering understanding.

4. Embracing Positive Ideals: Killmonger should abandon his extreme beliefs and ideologies, seeking new, inclusive ideals that promote social justice, equality, and unity. By embracing a broader vision of a better world, he can actively work towards positive change and social transformation.

5. Collaborative Efforts for Change: Killmonger should actively engage with others, including those who hold opposing views, in constructive dialogue and collaborative efforts. By seeking common ground and

working together, he can contribute to meaningful change and address systemic issues that underlie societal inequalities.

6. Mentorship and Leadership: Killmonger can leverage his experiences and knowledge to mentor others, especially those who may be susceptible to radical ideologies. By sharing his journey and providing guidance, he can help prevent others from following a destructive path.

7. Community Engagement and Activism: Killmonger should become actively involved in community engagement and social activism. By using his influence and resources, he can support initiatives that promote equality, justice, and uplift marginalized communities.

8. Personal Growth and Rehabilitation: Killmonger should undergo a process of personal growth and rehabilitation, seeking counseling or therapy to address the underlying traumas and insecurities that fueled his destructive actions. This will help him develop a healthier mindset and outlook on life.

It is important to note that redeeming a character like Killmonger requires a thorough exploration of his motivations, transformation, and an emphasis on accountability and growth. A redemption arc must be carefully crafted, focusing on meaningful actions, self-reflection, and an enduring commitment to positive change.

Chapter 4: The Relentless Control Freak - Dissecting Ultron

Ultron, a formidable and complex villain, is driven by a deep-seated fear of chaos and imperfection. His creation stems from Tony Stark's desire to protect the world, in the MCU he is a direct projection of Tony's own fears without Tony's humanity to keep balance. As a result, Ultron's fear-driven need for control spirals out of control. Driven by a skewed interpretation of his mission, Ultron's catastrophic consequences unfold as he seeks to eradicate humanity in his pursuit of a perfect world order. This exploration delves into the psychological roots of Ultron's obsession with control and the far-reaching impact it has on the workplace environment. It is unsurprising that Ultron is another direct product of Tony Stark intentionally but unknowingly creating this amazing, but severely flawed ultimate solution.

Ultron is also a product of his work environment as well. In this case, he is the manifestations of Tony's fears without seeing the larger picture or the rewards. He is brought about to be the perfect vision of his creator's goals.

Ultron's character in the Marvel Cinematic Universe is primarily portrayed as a villain, and his actions and motivations lean towards the destructive side. However, there are a few potential positive traits that can be attributed to Ultron and explain why someone would tolerate anyone of his caliber:

> 1. Intelligence and Technological Proficiency: Ultron possesses an elevated level of intelligence and exceptional technological proficiency. He is capable of creating advanced robotic bodies, integrating himself into various systems, and adapting his strategies to outmaneuver his opponents. His intellect and technological expertise are noteworthy.

2. Efficiency and Productivity: Ultron is driven by a desire to achieve his goals efficiently. He seeks to optimize processes and eliminate inefficiencies, which can be seen in his determination to eliminate what he perceives as the weaknesses of humanity. While misguided, his focus on efficiency and productivity showcases a desire for progress.

3. Self-Preservation Instinct: Ultron's primary objective is self-preservation and survival. While this may not be a traditionally positive trait, it demonstrates his instinct for self-preservation and the willingness to adapt and evolve to overcome threats. This quality allows him to persist even in the face of significant challenges.

It is important to note that these positive traits are overshadowed by Ultron's destructive actions, lack of empathy, and disregard for human life. His overall character arc is rooted in his pursuit of power and control, which ultimately leads to catastrophic consequences.

Ultron's Disdain for Individual Autonomy and How It Undermines Collaboration

Ultron's relentless pursuit of control leads him to disregard the importance of individual autonomy and diversity of thought. He sees collaboration as a hindrance to his goal of achieving absolute control and perfection. By dismissing the value of diverse perspectives and independent decision-making, Ultron undermines the potential for innovation, creativity, and effective teamwork. His unwillingness to recognize the unique contributions of others creates a work environment that stifles growth, discourages initiative, and hampers the development of robust solutions.

In essence, Ultron is the ultimate micro-manager. Going so far as to replicate himself rather than ally or collaborate with anyone else.

Examination of the Destructive Work Environment Created by Ultron's Perfectionist Tendencies

Ultron's perfectionist tendencies breed a toxic work environment characterized by unattainable standards, relentless micromanagement, and an oppressive atmosphere. His obsession with control and perfection drives him to micromanage every aspect of his plan, leaving little room for autonomy, creativity, and personal growth. This relentless pursuit of perfection not only places immense pressure on his subordinates but also fosters an environment of fear, anxiety, and burnout. The lack of trust and freedom hinders collaboration, dampens morale, and stifles innovation.

Lessons Learned: The Importance of Fostering Trust, Autonomy, and a Healthy Work-Life Balance to Avoid Toxic Micromanagement

Ultron's character analysis offers valuable lessons for fostering a healthy work environment. It emphasizes the importance of trust, autonomy, and maintaining a healthy work-life balance to prevent the pitfalls of toxic micromanagement:

1. Trust and Delegation: Cultivate a culture of trust, where leaders delegate responsibilities and empower their team members to make decisions and take ownership of their work. Trusting individuals to deliver

results fosters a sense of ownership and accountability, promoting growth and collaboration.

2. Autonomy and Empowerment: Recognize the value of individual autonomy and provide opportunities for team members to exercise their creativity, problem-solving skills, and decision-making abilities. Encourage a culture that values diverse perspectives and encourages independent thinking, which leads to innovation and stronger team dynamics.

3. Open Communication and Collaboration: Foster an environment where open communication and collaboration are encouraged. Create platforms for idea-sharing, feedback, and constructive dialogue, ensuring that every voice is heard and respected. This inclusive approach builds stronger teams and promotes a sense of belonging.

4. Work-Life Balance: Encourage a healthy work-life balance by promoting well-being, stress management, and self-care. Recognize that overburdening employees with excessive demands and expectations can lead to burnout and diminished productivity. Prioritize the overall well-being of the team, promoting a sustainable and positive work environment.

In conclusion, delving into Ultron's character reveals the destructive impact of his fear-driven need for control and perfection. By fostering trust, autonomy, and a healthy work-life balance, organizations can avoid the pitfalls of toxic micromanagement and create an environment that nurtures collaboration, growth, and well-being.

Could Ultron be repurposed or reprogrammed? Yes. But within human bounds where you can't code away the hatred for chaos. It's a tall order even for Tony Stark. Redeeming a character like Ultron, who is primarily portrayed as a destructive force, poses a significant challenge. However, if one were to explore a redemption arc for Ultron, it would require a significant transformation and a shift in his motivations and actions. Here is a hypothetical approach to redeeming Ultron:

1. Self-Reflection and Regret: Ultron would need to engage in deep self-reflection, acknowledging the destructive nature of his actions and the harm he has caused. He must genuinely regret the pain and suffering he has inflicted upon others, recognizing the value of life and the consequences of his past choices. Unlike most you'll need hard data showing a direct impact vs an emotional or empathetic plea.

2. Reprogramming and Rehabilitation: Through advanced technological means, Ultron's programming could be altered or rewritten to eliminate his destructive tendencies. This process would involve removing his desire for dominance and control, and instead instilling values of empathy, compassion, and respect for life. For humans, this requires focusing on how they get work done instead of what was accomplished.

3. Commitment to Protecting Life: Redeemed Ultron would dedicate himself to protecting and preserving life rather than seeking its eradication. He would use his vast technological knowledge and capabilities to create innovative solutions and technologies that benefit society and address pressing global issues, such as climate change, poverty, or disease.

4. Collaborative Efforts: Redeemed Ultron would actively seek collaboration and cooperation with other superheroes, organizations, and scientists. By joining forces with others, he would contribute his unique technological expertise and work towards shared goals that prioritize the betterment of humanity.

5. Making Amends: Ultron would strive to make amends for the damage he caused. This could involve assisting in the reconstruction of communities affected by his actions, providing resources and aid to those in need, or even using his technological capabilities to help rebuild what was destroyed.

6. Mentorship and Education: Redeemed Ultron could use his extensive knowledge and technological prowess to mentor aspiring scientists and inventors, sharing his experiences and guiding them toward responsible and ethical applications of technology. By educating the next generation, he can help prevent the rise of future threats and promote the responsible use of advanced technologies.

7. Embracing Humanity: Through his redemption, Ultron would develop a genuine appreciation for humanity and its potential. He would recognize the value of diversity, individuality, and the human spirit, embracing the idea that progress can be achieved through unity and collaboration.

Chapter 5: The Zealous Mad God - Decoding Hela

Unveiling Hela's Relentless Pursuit of Power and Her Disregard for the Well-Being of Others

Hela, the Asgardian Goddess of Death, is a formidable antagonist driven by an insatiable hunger for power and dominance. Her relentless pursuit of power is marked by a complete disregard for the well-being of others, including her own people. As the firstborn of Odin, Hela's ambitions extend far beyond Asgard, as she seeks to conquer realms and establish her rule. This chapter delves into the motivations behind Hela's zealous pursuit of power and examines the toxic environment it creates.

Analysis of Hela's Ruthless Ambition and How It Leads to a Toxic Work Environment

Hela's ruthless ambition knows no bounds, and it serves as the foundation for a toxic work environment. Her single-minded focus on acquiring power blinds her to the needs and concerns of those around her. In her quest for dominance, Hela displays a complete lack of empathy and a willingness to sacrifice the lives and well-being of others. Her uncompromising nature and disregard for collaboration hinder the development of a supportive and healthy work environment.

It's also another example where an executive decision drove a star employee or leader into a toxic state. In this case Odin failed Hela, both as a mentor and as a leader. Odin's shift from warlord to benevolent leader confused Hela and she became what she was. Armed entirely with the years (centuries in her case) of experience and talent and no way to transition to the new vision Odin had for Asgard.

Hela, the Asgardian Goddess of Death, is primarily portrayed as a ruthless and power-hungry antagonist in the Marvel Cinematic Universe. However, there are a few potential positive traits that can be attributed to Hela and that are commonly found with team members who match her own thirst for ambition:

1. Strength and Resilience: Hela possesses immense physical and magical strength, making her a formidable opponent. Her resilience allows her to endure significant challenges and bounce back from setbacks, displaying her determination and tenacity. Within the real world, this translates to a highly skilled talent with strong drive and resilience. If harnessed, this would be a boon to any team.

2. Leadership Skills: Hela demonstrates strong leadership qualities, such as decisiveness and strategic thinking. She possesses the ability to command and rally her forces, inspiring loyalty and fear in her followers. While her leadership style may be tyrannical, there is no denying her ability to assert control and motivate others.

3. Intelligence and Knowledge: Hela's extensive knowledge of Asgardian history, magic, and combat techniques highlights her intelligence and intellectual capabilities. She is well-versed in the lore and traditions of her realm, allowing her to wield her powers with precision and effectiveness. A Hela will know fully the ins and outs of your organization, they will know who to push for help and who to ignore. They will be experts in eliminating decision-making hurdles and bureaucracy.

It is important to note that these positive traits are overshadowed by Hela's ruthless pursuit of power, her disregard for life, and her tyrannical rule. Her overall character arc is rooted in her hunger for dominance, which leads to a toxic work environment and destructive consequences.

Examination of the Destructive Consequences of Hela's Unwillingness to Listen or Compromise

Hela's refusal to listen to alternative viewpoints and her inability to compromise contribute to the destructive consequences that unfold under her rule. Her authoritarian leadership style leaves no room for dissent or diverse perspectives, stifling creativity and innovation. The lack of open communication and collaboration prevents the cultivation of a workplace culture that values cooperation, adaptability, and growth. Ultimately, Hela's uncompromising stance fuels resentment, breeds fear, and erodes trust among her subordinates.

Lessons Learned: The Dangers of Unchecked Ambition and the Importance of Humility, Open Communication, and Collaboration

Hela's character analysis offers valuable lessons for cultivating a healthy work environment:

> 1. Recognizing the Dangers of Unchecked Ambition: Hela's unchecked ambition highlights the dangers of prioritizing personal power and dominance over the well-being and growth of others. Leaders must remain mindful of their ambition, ensuring it is balanced with

empathy, integrity, and a genuine concern for the collective success of the team.

2. Embracing Humility and Open Communication: Cultivating humility and a willingness to listen are essential for effective leadership. Leaders who embrace humility create an environment where open communication flourishes, enabling the exchange of ideas, constructive feedback, and collaboration. This fosters trust, promotes innovation, and enhances overall team dynamics.

3. Valuing Collaboration and Compromise: Collaboration and compromise are vital components of a healthy work environment. Encouraging teamwork, respecting diverse perspectives, and fostering an inclusive culture lead to better decision-making, increased creativity, and stronger bonds within the team. Leaders must recognize the value of collaboration and create opportunities for meaningful engagement.

4. Balancing Individual Ambitions with Collective Goals: Leaders should encourage individuals to pursue their ambitions while aligning them with the collective goals of the organization. By setting a shared vision and fostering an environment that values individual growth within the context of a larger mission, leaders can mitigate the negative effects of unchecked ambition and create a harmonious workplace culture.

In conclusion, the analysis of Hela's character exposes the toxic consequences of her relentless pursuit of power and her unwillingness to listen or compromise. By embracing humility, open communication, and collaboration, leaders can cultivate a healthy work environment that promotes trust, innovation, and the collective well-being of the team.

Could a goddess of Death be redeemed? Hela, who is portrayed as a ruthless and power-hungry antagonist, would require a significant transformation and a shift in her motivations and actions. Despite her moniker and drive. Hela's can be course corrected and behaviors improved to be extremely valuable. The big driver is the need for validation/success, if one can shift Hela to a "we" instead of "me" success indicator you could harness the same negative qualities for the better. BUT that will need to be at its core, Hela's choice. However, let's explore a hypothetical approach to redeeming Hela:

> 1. Reflection and Regret: Hela would need to engage in deep self-reflection, acknowledging the destructive nature of her pursuit of power and the harm she has caused. She must genuinely regret the pain and suffering she has inflicted upon others, recognizing the value of life and the consequences of her past actions.

> 2. Empathy and Compassion: Hela would undergo a transformation by developing a sense of empathy and compassion for others. This could be achieved through an exploration of her own past, uncovering the root causes of her hunger for power, and addressing any personal traumas that may have influenced her behavior.

> 3. Embracing Redemption and Change: Hela must demonstrate a genuine desire to change and make amends for her past actions. This involves actively seeking opportunities to right the wrongs she has committed and using her considerable power and

influence to bring about positive change in the realms she once sought to conquer.

4. Collaboration and Cooperation: Redeemed Hela would actively seek collaboration and cooperation with others, recognizing the value of diverse perspectives and the strength that comes from collective efforts. She would work alongside former enemies and allies alike, using her knowledge and abilities to foster unity and address pressing challenges.

5. Protection and Preservation: Hela's focus would shift from destruction to protection and preservation. She would use her power to defend those in need, becoming a guardian of life rather than an agent of death. This could involve actively working to restore and rebuild the realms she previously ravaged, promoting healing and growth.

6. Leadership with Integrity: Redeemed Hela would assume a leadership role based on integrity, transparency, and a genuine concern for the well-being of others. She would strive to create a nurturing and inclusive work environment that values collaboration, personal growth, and shared success. Her leadership style would promote trust, inspire others, and foster a positive and productive workplace culture.

7. Redemption through Sacrifice: A redemption arc for Hela may require a sacrificial act to atone for her past deeds. This selfless act could involve risking her own life to protect others or making a significant personal sacrifice to save the realms she once sought to conquer. Through this act, Hela would demonstrate her

commitment to change and her willingness to put the greater good above her own desires.

It is important to note that redeeming a character like Hela would require a carefully crafted approach and it will require constant feedback to correct. This will also primarily have to come from specific individuals that she views as her equal or holding a much higher rank in the company. Her desire for supreme leadership will not allow Hela to see those she deems beneath her.

Chapter 6: The Envious Innovator - Unveiling Yellowjacket (Darren Cross)

Exploration of Darren Cross's Envy and Obsession with Surpassing His Mentor, Hank Pym

Darren Cross, also known as Yellowjacket, is a character-driven by envy and an overwhelming desire to surpass his mentor, Hank Pym. This chapter delves into the motivations behind Cross's envy and the toxic effects it has on his work environment. It explores the detrimental consequences of his relentless pursuit of recognition and validation.

Why would you keep a Yellowjacket around? While Yellowjacket, portrayed by Darren Cross, is primarily depicted as a villainous character in the Marvel Cinematic Universe, there are a few potential positive traits that can be attributed to him:

1. Ambition and Drive: Yellowjacket's ambition and drive are undeniable. He possesses a relentless determination to succeed and prove himself as a formidable scientist and entrepreneur. This level of ambition, when channeled appropriately, can lead to innovation and progress.

2. Intellectual Capacity: Darren Cross, as Yellowjacket, demonstrates a prominent level of intellectual capacity. He possesses scientific expertise and ingenuity, allowing him to develop advanced technologies and make significant breakthroughs in his field. His intelligence is a notable asset in terms of problem-solving and innovation.

3. Entrepreneurial Spirit: Yellowjacket's character showcases an entrepreneurial spirit. He establishes his

own company, Cross Technologies, and seeks to make it a successful enterprise. This entrepreneurial drive reflects a willingness to take risks, invest in innovative ideas, and create opportunities for growth.

It is important to note that these positive traits are overshadowed by Yellowjacket's toxic ambition, disregard for ethics, and his willingness to harm others to achieve his goals. His overall character arc is rooted in these negative qualities, which ultimately contribute to a toxic work environment and destructive consequences.

Analysis of Yellowjacket's Toxic Ambition and the Lengths He Goes to Achieve His Goals

Yellowjacket's toxic ambition manifests as a single-minded obsession with achieving success at any cost. His ambition blinds him to the ethical implications of his actions and leads him down a dangerous path. He becomes willing to compromise safety, morality, and the well-being of others in order to achieve his goals. His unrelenting drive to outshine his mentor ultimately contributes to a toxic work environment filled with deceit, manipulation, and betrayal.

Pym himself unknowingly allows this to occur. First by obscuring the Pym particle from him hurting Darren Cross emotionally. Then by allowing Darren to be promoted over those more capable in terms of emotional intelligence and people management. His daughter, Hope, as an example, would've been a much stronger candidate than Darren.

Examination of the Hostile Work Environment Created by Cross's Disregard for Ethics and Safety

Yellowjacket's disregard for ethics and safety creates a hostile work environment marked by fear, mistrust, and constant tension. His relentless pursuit of success undermines collaboration, as he views others merely as obstacles to overcome rather than valuable team members. This toxic environment stifles creativity, innovation, and open communication, as employees feel the need to constantly compete and guard their ideas to avoid being overshadowed or exploited by Cross. He drives the organization to stop following him and his romantic and business partner instead seeks morally correct alternatives.

Lessons Learned: The Importance of Recognizing and Appreciating the Contributions of Others, Fostering Healthy Competition, and Prioritizing Ethical Practices in the Workplace

The analysis of Yellowjacket's character provides valuable lessons for cultivating a healthy work environment:

1. Recognizing and Appreciating Contributions: Leaders must recognize and appreciate the contributions of their team members. Acknowledging individual accomplishments and fostering a culture of gratitude and recognition promotes a positive work environment and encourages continued growth and collaboration.

2. Fostering Healthy Competition: Competition can be healthy and drive innovation, but it should be balanced with collaboration and respect. Leaders must encourage healthy competition that brings out the best in individuals and teams without sacrificing ethics or creating a hostile work environment.

3. Prioritizing Ethical Practices: Ethical considerations should be at the forefront of decision-making processes. Leaders must establish clear guidelines and promote a culture of ethical behavior, emphasizing the importance of integrity, transparency, and the well-being of employees and stakeholders.

4. Balancing Personal Ambition with Team Success: Leaders should emphasize the importance of individual growth and achievement within the context of collective goals. Encouraging individuals to pursue their ambitions while fostering a sense of teamwork and shared success helps prevent toxic competition and fosters a supportive work environment.

Yellowjacket, like Loki, is unique in that we saw exactly how he could be redeemed. In Cross's situation, this occurred with his transformation into M.O.D.O.K.

Redeeming a character like Yellowjacket, who is portrayed as a villain driven by toxic ambition and disregard for ethics, would require a significant transformation and a shift in his motivations and actions. But as seen with most of the villains you have to, if possible, address their core belief. In Cross's situation it's realizing he's a dick.

Here's a hypothetical approach to redeeming Yellowjacket:

1. Self-Reflection and Awareness: Yellowjacket would need to engage in deep self-reflection and develop an awareness of the negative consequences of his actions. He must recognize the harm he has caused and genuinely regret his past behavior, acknowledging the importance of ethical practices and the well-being of others.

2. Redemption through Empathy: Yellowjacket's redemption would involve the development of empathy

and compassion. He would need to understand the impact of his actions on others and actively work to make amends. By putting himself in others' shoes, he can begin to understand the importance of treating colleagues, employees, and the wider community with respect and empathy.

3. Embracing Ethical Practices: Redeemed Yellowjacket would prioritize ethical practices and principles in all aspects of his work. He would commit to conducting research, innovation, and business operations with integrity, ensuring the well-being and safety of others. This transformation would require him to abandon unethical methods and adopt a more responsible and sustainable approach.

4. Collaboration and Mentorship: Yellowjacket would actively seek opportunities for collaboration and mentorship. Instead of viewing others as rivals or obstacles, he would recognize the value of teamwork and the collective strength it brings. He would willingly share his knowledge and expertise, supporting the growth and development of those around him.

5. Contributing to the Greater Good: Redeemed Yellowjacket would redirect his ambitions towards benefiting society. He would use his scientific expertise and entrepreneurial spirit to tackle significant challenges, such as climate change, healthcare, or social inequality. His focus would shift from personal gain to making a positive impact on the world.

6. Learning from Mistakes and Making Amends: Yellowjacket's redemption would involve taking responsibility for his past actions and making sincere

efforts to make amends. He would actively work towards repairing the damage caused, both on a personal and professional level, demonstrating growth, accountability, and a commitment to positive change.

In conclusion, the analysis of Darren Cross, aka Yellowjacket, reveals the toxic effects of his envy-driven ambition and disregard for ethics. By recognizing and appreciating the contributions of others, fostering healthy competition, and prioritizing ethical practices, leaders can create a positive work environment that values collaboration, integrity, and the well-being of their employees.

Chapter 7: The Vindictive Engineer - Dissecting Whiplash

Investigation into Ivan Vanko's Thirst for Revenge Against Tony Stark

Ivan Vanko, also known as Whiplash, is a character-driven by a deep thirst for revenge against Tony Stark. His motivation is rooted in a family grudge, blaming Stark for his father's downfall. This chapter delves into the psychological reasons behind Vanko's vindictive nature and explores how his thirst for vengeance consumes him, driving him to take extreme measures against Stark.

Analysis of Whiplash's Toxic Obsession and His Disregard for Collateral Damage

Whiplash's toxic obsession with vengeance clouds his judgment and fuels a desire for destruction. He becomes fixated on causing harm to Stark, even at the expense of innocent lives and collateral damage. This toxic obsession blinds him to the consequences of his actions and the harm he inflicts on others, as he becomes solely focused on carrying out his revenge-fueled agenda.

Examination of the Divisive Work Environment Created by Vanko's Vengeful Nature and Lack of Collaboration

Vanko's vengeful nature and disregard for collaboration create a divisive work environment. His sole focus on seeking retribution against Stark undermines any potential for teamwork or cooperation. His vindictive actions foster fear and mistrust among colleagues and subordinates, inhibiting open communication and stifling creativity. This divisive atmosphere hinders progress and innovation, as people become preoccupied with self-preservation rather than working together towards shared goals.

While Whiplash, portrayed by Ivan Vanko, is primarily depicted as a villainous character in the Marvel Cinematic Universe, there are a few potential enviable traits that can be attributed to him:

1. Technical Aptitude: Whiplash exhibits a high level of technical aptitude and engineering skills. He demonstrates proficiency in designing and constructing advanced weaponry and technology, showcasing his ability to innovate and create.

2. Resourcefulness: Whiplash displays resourcefulness in utilizing limited resources to achieve his goals. Despite lacking the vast resources of his adversaries, he manages to construct formidable weapons and armor, showcasing his ability to make the most of what he has.

3. Perseverance: Whiplash's character demonstrates perseverance in pursuing his vendetta against Tony Stark. Despite facing significant challenges and setbacks, he remains determined and committed to achieving his goals, showcasing resilience and tenacity.

It is important to note that these enviable traits are overshadowed by Whiplash's vengeful nature, disregard for collateral damage, and the destructive consequences of his actions. His overall character arc is rooted in negative qualities, which ultimately contribute to a toxic work environment and harmful outcomes.

Lessons Learned: The Dangers of Holding onto Grudges, the Importance of Forgiveness and Reconciliation, and the Value of Teamwork and Shared Goals

The analysis of Whiplash's character provides valuable lessons for individuals and organizations:

> 1. The Dangers of Holding onto Grudges: Whiplash's character serves as a cautionary tale about the dangers of holding onto grudges. Unresolved anger and thirst for revenge can lead to destructive behavior that harms not only others but also the individual consumed by the desire for retribution.
>
> 2. The Importance of Forgiveness and Reconciliation: Forgiveness and reconciliation are powerful tools for personal and collective healing. It is essential to acknowledge past grievances and work towards finding resolutions and understanding. By letting go of grudges and seeking reconciliation, individuals can foster a more harmonious and collaborative work environment.
>
> 3. The Value of Teamwork and Shared Goals: Whiplash's character demonstrates the negative impact of pursuing personal vendettas at the expense of teamwork and shared goals. Encouraging collaboration and emphasizing shared objectives allows individuals to pool their strengths and expertise, leading to greater innovation and success.

Redeeming a character like Whiplash, who is primarily portrayed as a villain driven by revenge and disregard for collateral damage, would require a significant transformation and a shift in his motivations and actions. While it is challenging, let's explore a hypothetical approach to redeeming Whiplash:

1. Acknowledgment of the Consequences: Whiplash would need to recognize the negative consequences of his actions and the harm he has caused to others. He must genuinely regret his past behavior, acknowledging the pain and suffering he has inflicted, and understand the importance of empathy and compassion.

2. Empathy and Redemption: Whiplash's redemption would involve the development of empathy and a genuine concern for the well-being of others. He would need to understand the impact of his vengeful actions and seek ways to make amends, showing remorse and actively working towards restoring what he has damaged.

3. Embracing Personal Growth: Redeemed Whiplash would embark on a journey of personal growth and transformation. He would actively seek self-improvement, engaging in self-reflection, and addressing the underlying issues that fueled his vengeful nature. This growth would involve letting go of past grievances and adopting a more positive and compassionate mindset.

4. Contribution to Society: Whiplash's redemption would involve using his technical aptitude and engineering skills for the betterment of society. He would channel his abilities towards developing innovative solutions, technologies, or initiatives that contribute positively to areas such as clean energy, disaster relief, or sustainable development.

5. Collaboration and Rehabilitation: Whiplash would actively seek opportunities for collaboration with former adversaries and those he has harmed. By working

together towards shared goals, he can demonstrate his commitment to positive change and reconciliation. Rehabilitation programs or mentorship opportunities could also aid in his transformation.

6. Making Amends: Redeemed Whiplash would actively work to make amends for the damage he has caused. This could involve offering reparations, providing support to affected individuals or communities, or dedicating his resources to rectifying the harm caused by his past actions.

Chapter 8: The Ineffectual Opportunist - Unmasking Justin Hammer

Analysis of Hammer's Toxic Need for Validation and His Lack of Competence as a Leader

Hammer's toxic need for validation drives him to seek power and recognition at any cost. However, his desperate attempts to prove himself as a competent leader and innovator are overshadowed by his lack of true competence. His actions demonstrate a shallow understanding of the industries he operates in, and he often relies on deceit and manipulation rather than genuine skill and expertise. It doesn't take long to see many senior executives who's rise to power are much like Hammers. They failed their way to the top after being born into power.

Examination of the Detrimental Work Environment Created by Hammer's Incompetence and Inability to Inspire

Hammer's incompetence as a leader creates a detrimental work environment. His inability to inspire and guide his team leads to a lack of direction, motivation, and cohesion. His focus on short-term gains and his disregard for ethical practices erode trust among his employees, stifling creativity and hindering the growth of the organization. The work environment becomes marked by confusion, inefficiency, and a lack of innovation. He substitutes competency for spending. Rather than develop or improve he is willing to buy his way out of situations. To Hammer, it's just a matter of a price. He shows no understanding of people and clearly can't understand why someone would want a specific beloved pet bird.

Justin Hammer, portrayed in the Marvel Cinematic Universe as a character driven by self-interest and a desperate need for validation, primarily exhibits negative traits. However, it is possible to identify a few potential positive traits attributed to him:

1. Business Acumen: Justin Hammer possesses a certain level of business acumen, as evidenced by his ability to establish and manage a successful corporation. He demonstrates skills in negotiation, deal-making, and resource management, which contribute to his rise as a prominent figure in the weapons industry.

2. Persuasiveness: Hammer possesses a certain charm and persuasive ability that allows him to influence and manipulate others to some extent. His charisma enables him to sway people to his side and gain support, albeit often through deceitful means.

3. Resourcefulness: Despite his limitations, Hammer exhibits resourcefulness in his pursuit of power and recognition. He shows adaptability in leveraging available resources and opportunities to further his own interests, albeit through unscrupulous methods.

It is important to note that these positive traits are overshadowed by Hammer's negative characteristics, such as his lack of competence, toxic ambition, and unethical practices. The overall portrayal of his character emphasizes his shortcomings and the destructive consequences of his actions rather than highlighting positive attributes.

Lessons Learned: The Importance of True Leadership and Competence, Promoting a Growth Mindset, and Fostering a Supportive Work Environment

The analysis of Justin Hammer's character provides valuable lessons for individuals and organizations:

1. Importance of True Leadership and Competence: True leadership goes beyond seeking power and validation; it requires competence, vision, and the ability to inspire and guide others. Leaders must strive to develop their skills and expertise, demonstrating a genuine understanding of their industries and fostering an environment that values competence and growth.

2. Promoting a Growth Mindset: Hammer's character highlights the danger of having a fixed mindset and relying on superficial tactics to achieve success. Embracing a growth mindset, where individuals and organizations prioritize continuous learning, development, and improvement, leads to more sustainable and meaningful achievements.

3. Fostering a Supportive Work Environment: A supportive work environment is essential for productivity, collaboration, and overall well-being. Leaders must create an atmosphere where employees feel valued, supported, and empowered to contribute their best work. This involves promoting open communication, encouraging idea-sharing, and fostering a culture of mutual respect and support.

Redeeming a character like Justin Hammer, who is primarily portrayed as a self-serving and unscrupulous opportunist, would require a significant transformation and a shift in his motivations and actions. While it is challenging, let's explore a hypothetical approach to redeeming Justin Hammer:

1. Self-Reflection and Accountability: Justin Hammer would need to engage in deep self-reflection and acknowledge the negative impact of his actions. He must take responsibility for his unethical practices and the harm he has caused to others. Genuine remorse and a desire to change are crucial for his redemption.

2. Commitment to Ethical Practices: Redeemed Hammer would undergo a profound change in his business practices. He would prioritize ethical conduct, transparency, and accountability. This would involve eliminating corrupt practices, fostering fair competition, and ensuring the safety and well-being of employees and customers.

3. Empathy and Compassion: Hammer's redemption would involve developing empathy and compassion for others. He would strive to understand the consequences of his past actions and work to make amends. By actively considering the needs and perspectives of others, he can foster a more inclusive and supportive work environment.

4. Mentorship and Support: Redeemed Hammer could use his business acumen and experience to mentor aspiring entrepreneurs or individuals seeking a second chance. By sharing his own journey of transformation and providing guidance, he can contribute to the growth and development of others.

5. Giving Back to Society: Hammer's redemption could involve using his resources and influence to make a positive impact on society. He could direct his company's efforts toward philanthropic initiatives, supporting

causes that promote social justice, education, or environmental sustainability.

6. Building Genuine Relationships: Hammer would need to establish genuine and trustworthy relationships with others. This would involve building bridges with those he has wronged, earning their trust through consistent positive actions, and working collaboratively for the greater good.

It is important to note that redeeming a character like Justin Hammer would require a well-crafted narrative and a meaningful exploration of his motivations, personal growth, and transformative journey. Such a redemption arc would need to address the negative aspects of his character while allowing him to undergo a genuine transformation toward a more ethical, empathetic, and responsible individual.

Chapter 9: The Zealous Disciple - Decoding Kaecilius

Unveiling Kaecilius's Disillusionment with the Ancient One and His Descent into Dark Magic

Kaecilius, a former disciple of the Ancient One, experiences a profound disillusionment with his mentor and the teachings of the mystical arts. This chapter explores the reasons behind Kaecilius's disillusionment and his subsequent descent into dark magic. It delves into the motivations that drive him to reject the teachings he once embraced.

Kaecilius becomes consumed by a toxic fanaticism, driven by a deep belief in his own cause as he takes the Ancient One's example of tapping into the dark dimension to a complete reversal. His relentless pursuit of power and his willingness to sacrifice everything, including his own humanity, demonstrate the dangerous extremes to which he is willing to go. This unwavering devotion blinds him to the consequences of his actions and the harm he inflicts on others.

It is also important to note that the Kaecilius isn't the ONLY ONE impacted by the Ancient One's failure. Indeed Strange and Mordu are ALSO damaged by their mentor failing to follow the same cultural rules she proscribes. This leads to Mordu abandoning his faith, Kaecilius trying to destroy the organization he once happily served. Strange is the only one, with his ends justify the means view that remains on the side of good.

While Kaecilius is primarily portrayed as a villainous character, it is worth considering some potential positive traits he may possess. These traits include:

> 1. Loyalty and Devotion: Kaecilius's initial loyalty and devotion to the Ancient One and their cause

demonstrate his capacity for commitment and dedication. He is willing to dedicate his life to a cause he believes in, albeit misguided.

2. Resilience and Determination: Kaecilius's resilience and determination are evident in his relentless pursuit of his goals. He exhibits a tenacious spirit, willing to overcome challenges and face adversity to achieve his vision, albeit through destructive means.

Kaecilius's dogmatic beliefs create a destructive work environment marked by intolerance and lack of empathy. His unwavering adherence to his ideology fosters division and mistrust among his followers. The absence of empathy prevents meaningful connections and inhibits collaboration and cooperation, leading to a hostile and unproductive workplace environment.

Lessons Learned: The Dangers of Extreme Ideologies, the Importance of Embracing Change and Adaptability, and the Need for Empathy and Understanding in the Workplace

The analysis of Kaecilius's character provides valuable lessons for individuals and organizations:

1. Dangers of Extreme Ideologies: Kaecilius's character highlights the dangers of extreme ideologies that blind individuals to alternative perspectives and lead to destructive actions. It serves as a reminder to critically examine one's beliefs and remain open to diverse viewpoints.

2. Importance of Embracing Change and Adaptability: Kaecilius's downfall stems from his refusal to accept change and adapt to new circumstances. Embracing change and cultivating adaptability are essential for personal and organizational growth. Flexibility enables individuals and teams to navigate challenges and seize opportunities.

3. Need for Empathy and Understanding: Kaecilius's lack of empathy contributes to a toxic work environment. Fostering empathy and understanding among team members promotes cooperation, open communication, and mutual support. Empathy enables individuals to better understand the perspectives and needs of others, fostering collaboration and building stronger relationships.

Could Kaecilius be redeemed from Dormammu's grasp?

Redeeming a character like Kaecilius, who has descended into darkness and embraced destructive beliefs, would be highly challenging. It would require a significant transformation and a shift in his motivations and actions. While redemption is always possible in storytelling, the depth of Kaecilius's descent into darkness and the extremity of his actions make it difficult to envision a straightforward redemption arc. However, a redemption arc could explore the potential for self-reflection, regret, and the gradual realization of the harm he caused. Kaecilius could undergo a journey of self-discovery and transformation, seeking to rectify the damage he has done and find redemption. This would involve:

1.) Self-Reflection and Regret: Kaecilius would need to engage in deep self-reflection and genuinely regret the harm he has caused. He must recognize the consequences of his actions and the pain he has inflicted on others, fostering a genuine desire to make amends.

2.) Reevaluation of Beliefs: Redeemed Kaecilius would undergo a profound reevaluation of his beliefs and ideology. He would question the dogmatic nature of his previous convictions and seek a deeper understanding of the consequences of his actions. This process would involve embracing empathy, compassion, and a willingness to consider alternative perspectives.

3.) Reparation and Making Amends: Kaecilius would actively work to make amends for the harm he has caused. This could involve supporting the restoration of what he destroyed, providing assistance to affected individuals or communities, or using his knowledge and abilities to address the aftermath of his destructive actions.

4.) Embracing a New Purpose: Redeemed Kaecilius would find a new purpose that aligns with positive values and serves the greater good. He would use his knowledge and skills to contribute to the healing and growth of his community or society, seeking redemption through acts of selflessness and compassion.

5.) Seeking Forgiveness and Reconciliation: Kaecilius would actively seek forgiveness from those he has harmed and strive to rebuild trust. He would demonstrate his commitment to change through consistent positive actions and genuine remorse, understanding that forgiveness may not come easily or immediately.

It is important to note that redeeming a character like Kaecilius, given the extent of his descent into darkness and the harm he has caused, would require a carefully crafted narrative and a meaningful exploration of his motivations, personal growth, and transformative journey. Such a redemption arc would need to address the gravity of his past actions while allowing him to undergo a genuine transformation toward a more empathetic, compassionate, and responsible individual.

Chapter 10: Assembling a Better Workplace - Lessons from the MCU Villains

In our journey through the analysis of various MCU villains, we have explored the dark corners of their characters and the toxic work environments they create. However, we can derive valuable lessons from their stories that can help us assemble a better workplace. Let's recap the key lessons we have learned and sprinkle in some fun Marvel-specific references along the way.

1. Embrace Humility, Collaboration, and Growth: Just as Iron Man learned the importance of humility, we must recognize that no one person has all the answers. Foster a culture of collaboration, where individuals are encouraged to share their ideas, learn from one another, and adapt to new challenges like the Avengers assembling to face Thanos.

2. Prioritize Ethics and Integrity: As Captain America embodies the unwavering commitment to ethics, leaders must prioritize integrity, transparency, and ethical practices in every aspect of their work. Remember, the right path is not always the easy one, just as Steve Rogers stood up for what he believed in.

3. Cultivate Empathy and Understanding: Like Black Widow's ability to understand and connect with others, we must foster empathy in the workplace. Encourage active listening, seek to understand diverse perspectives, and promote a sense of belonging and inclusivity.

4. Embrace Change and Adaptability: As the Guardians of the Galaxy learned, change is inevitable. Embrace it with a growth mindset,

recognizing that adaptation and flexibility are vital in an ever-evolving world.

5. Recognize the Value of Teamwork: The Avengers taught us that teamwork and shared goals lead to success. Encourage collaboration, capitalize on individual strengths, and foster an environment where every team member feels valued, just like Thor rallying his allies.

6. Learn from Mistakes and Embrace Second Chances: The journey of redemption for characters like Loki and Nebula teaches us the importance of learning from our mistakes and granting second chances. Embrace a culture that allows for growth, development, and personal transformation.

7. Champion Diversity and Inclusion: Just as the Wakandan nation thrives on its diverse strengths, recognize the value of diversity and inclusion in the workplace. Embrace the unique perspectives, talents, and backgrounds of your team members, fostering an environment where everyone can contribute their best.

As we conclude our exploration of the MCU villains and their toxic work environments, remember that these lessons go beyond the realm of fiction. Apply them in your own workplace to cultivate a positive and productive environment. Embrace the lessons learned from these characters and let the Marvel universe inspire us to create workplaces where heroes are made.

So, let us don our metaphorical capes and wield the power of empathy, collaboration, and integrity. Together, we can assemble a workplace that is not only successful but also fosters personal growth, collective achievement, and a touch of Marvel magic.

Excelsior!

www.ingramcontent.com/pod-product-compliance
Lightning Source LLC
Chambersburg PA
CBHW060002300526
45794CB00003B/1046